So Runs the Water

~ life's journey, in verse ~

by

Tom Mach

~ Books by Tom Mach ~

Fiction
- SISSY!
- ALL PARTS TOGETHER
- ANGELS AT SUNSET
- STORIES TO ENJOY
- THE INVISIBLE TWINS
- THE ADVENTURES OF HOMER THE ROAMER

Memoir
- PERSISTENCE, THEN PEACE

Poetry
- THE UNI VERSE
- THE MUSEUM MUSE
- SO RUNS THE WATER

NOTE: If you would like to contact Tom Mach you can find his email address by clicking on www.Tom-Mach.com

SO RUNS THE WATER

Acknowledgement given to http://wallpaperswide.com/ for use of Its photos on front and back

Library of Congress Control Number: 2017906591
ISBN: 978-0-6928830-3-7

Published by

Hill Song Press
Lawrence, KS

HILL SONG PRESS
Lawrence, KS 66044
www.HillSongPress.com

"You can never step into the same river twice."

~ Heracticus,
5th century BC Greek philosopher

Why I Wrote About Water

If bread is the staff of life, water is its necessary accompaniment. Human beings and animals can't exist without it. Nonetheless, water is something many of us take for granted. Some of us may not realize that there is also a spiritual dimension to water, which I bring out in this poetry book.

Actually, I wanted to write an ode about water, much like I previously wanted to write an ode about the universe—which had resulted in not just an ode, but an award-winning collection of poetry called *The Uni Verse*.

I titled this book *So Runs the Water* because water runs through our lives in so many different ways. Our lives are amorphous; they move and change from day to day, month to year, and year to year. Running water is also amorphous. If we were to take a sample of creek water every hour, for example, and analyze its mineral content, we would find no two samples exactly alike. The same thing goes for the design of snowflakes. No two are ever exactly alike.

When I was a student of chemical engineering, I learned the formulae for predicting the changing flow resistance of water traveling through different types and sizes of pipes. In my senior year I did an experiment where I measured the heat transfer effect when baffles are used in an agitated tank of water. But while my left brain appreciated the science behind it, my right brain only felt fulfilled when I sat at an ocean beach, watching the surf slap against the rocks. It was both beautiful and terrifying at the same time—beautiful the way its splendor and innocence added to the scene, and terrifying because of its capacity for destruction. That is why I decided to write about water.

It is a physical thing. It is a spiritual thing.

So Runs the Water
~ life's journey, in verse ~

by Tom Mach

So runs the water

churning at times,

forming white circles,

foaming as if angry,

pushing against craggy rocks,

crushing them to sand—

not all at once,

but over eons of time,

as it forms new land boundaries,

new beaches,

new beachheads,

new streams,

new rivers.

So runs the water,

spinning whirls of molecules,

slipping and sliding about,

oxygen married to hydrogen pairs.

In its simplicity it hides its terror,

crushing buildings, smashing trees

In its simplicity it hides its peace,

baptizing sinners,

washing hands,

cooling bodies

So runs the water,

forming rivulets,

then streams,

then rivers.

then oceans.

Waters that fondle canoes

and support aircraft carriers.

Large rivers that sweep under bridges

and carry soldiers to battle.

Oceans that also carry soldiers to battle

to later serve some with gentle coffins.

So runs the water,

stubborn in its decided direction,

yet moving with peaceful grace

while holding an arrogant white swan

with the care of a loving mother.

All is movement above the bridge.

Nightingales fly from tangled tree limbs,

an adagio of heaven floats in a dark sky.

All is song as the river flows gently,

unaware of the roaring falls ahead.

So runs the water,

pouring like thunder from falls,

spilling over immense concrete walls,

spinning rotors of giant generators

Honeymooners at Niagara Falls

marvel at its white foam, crashing booms,

majestic power finally unleashed.

Later, a wall switch turns on the light.

So runs the water,

arising into clouds,

growing, populating,

forming a white canvas,

daring to hide the sun,

until the canvas is shaken,

spewing electrical flashes

and pounding thunder

and rain.

So runs the water,

praised by farmers,

cursed by city folk.

Yet even they know

they need rain

to appreciate sunshine,

to give them an excuse

to work indoors or

to sleep to pitter-patter.

So runs the water

going down a drain

in circular fashion.

In lakes and rivers

eddies swirl

with the current.

A fishing reel

spins noisily

with a hooked bass.

A lighthouse beacon

circles slowly about,

across midnight waters.

So runs the water,

taking on different roles,

and in different venues,

similar to the human theater.

Humans too take on diverse roles,

although each role dubbed unique.

It is as if we are in dress rehearsal

for something extraordinary.

We act out our parts

while the Director sits quietly

in the far corner of a room,

taking notes.

It is time for us to take a rest

and prepare for a new role

in the next play.

Water also takes on many roles

in many forms of running,

pounding rain, scorching steam,

thundering waterfall, angry ocean.

But peace and stillness is its best role.

~ the immense sea

There is something mystical about the sea,

especially the Sea of Galilee.

At one time, Jesus walked on it.

During a storm, He ordered it to be calm.

The world's seas drown us with their beauty.

Artists have painted them.

Poets have praised them.

Yet none can really capture their splendor.

Thrown on the reefs of the land

are washings of forgotten loves,

of children romping o'er the waves,

of adults splashing with aplomb,

hopping on boards to challenge the sea,

running out their old boats,

hoping for a net grab of shrimp,

unaware they also catch the waters

that washed the skins of forgotten men.

Vikings, pirates, and the once-famous,

as well as the vast unknown of us—

the ones who thought they'd live forever

but were swallowed by the deep.

The immense sea, shown from afar

is what gives the earth its luster.

Yes, earth, polished blue orb,

spinning souls to day and night,

rounding massive star.

~ *the moon*

That massive star retreats from view,

and though it pulls a black curtain sky,

it leaves behind a round, white lamp,

an orb praised by ancient lovers,

later written into music like

Beethoven's *Moonlight Sonata*,

wherein the composer clawed

rising notes

before falling in despair.

If only the moon would speak

what would it say?

Ah! Listen!

I am the Moon.

I have volcanic plains called seas

because ancient astronomers

mistook them for oceans,

yet some are vaster than yours.

I am the Moon.

I have witnessed dinosaurs

roaming your Earth.

and I have also seen the comet's

impact that destroyed them.

I am the Moon.

I gasped and wept

when a great flood covered your Earth,

and I wondered if your orb

would be devoid of life—like mine.

I am the Moon.

I was worshiped by the pharaohs as a god,

while the ancient Greeks called me a goddess.

I am the Moon.

I saw Galileo examine my craters

through a device called a telescope.

I am the Moon.

I have seen wars circling your globe

and questioned what you meant by peace.

I am the Moon.

I awoke to thumping of human footsteps

atop my Sea of Tranquility

with "one giant step for mankind".

I am the Moon.

I miss those days when lovers gazed upon me,

and when they composed songs in my name.

I am the Moon.

One day humans will explore the rest of me

and discover new seas.

~ clouds

Artists often paint a golden moon

hovering over a calm lake

But sometimes the moon

is obscured by sky pillows.

Yet in the day they soften the sky

and humor us with their shapes.

There is a cycle about clouds.

I've always known

that clouds bring rain

But as a young lad

I lay on a green mattress

of prickly blades of grass

and looked up at the sky

as clouds seem to float together

in perfect harmony.

When I am no longer six

I am told this happens

when the earth spins on its axis

and clouds don't float together

in perfect harmony.

I also believed rainbows

were miracles because they

were God's bow of remembrance

never to repeat the Great Flood

but it is also when I am no longer six

that I learn rainbows are caused

by light refracting through water droplets

~ open Your clouds, Lord

Science looks at the physical

while I look at the metaphysical.

Clouds are trillions of tiny droplets

Which form around dust particles.

But I disagree.

Clouds are God's comfort mattress.

Indeed, a cloud once guided

Moses through the wilderness

and hid the Father during

His Son's transfiguration.

(Open Your clouds, O Lord,

and let me taste heaven.

Open Your sky, O Lord,

and let me see the Word.

Open Your love, O Lord,

and let me die to myself.)

~ *winter*

Clouds are puffy and happy

in the summer,

but flat and treacherous

in the winter.

You say there is magic in winter?

Or is there something irritable about

frozen water dropping from the sky?

I look at winter through a peephole

of my frosted window pane.

There! See nature's canvas?

Through the lifeless tree limbs

the sun pierces the frozen dead

and oozes a golden halo

upon angel flakes of snow,

reminding me to be patient.

Spring will soon resurrect

as will we

after we are dead.

Rain, sleet, and snow

is nature's way of challenging us,

as drops of cold rain dot the landscape,

and the ice-glazed roads fight cars,

causing some to slide off the road.

The sky is an angry-gray

and the air dense with snowflakes.

Drivers turn on their car radios,

only to hear a weatherman drone on

about a predicted historic snowfall

but a few don't give a damn about that.

The hospital doors never close

as some saviors may be needed in ER today

to resuscitate the life of a dying child.

~ *children*

Children ought to be fascinated by a river

because of its twists and turns,

making them wonder

how the river knew where to change direction.

They also need to learn how the loam

 gently squeezes the living juices from the

earth's mantle, crowning it with rivulets

that add both joy and a new vision.

My grandson notices me staring at the woods.

The night is cool and quiet

and the lake is smooth

and as still as death,

but an occasional cricket

shatters the silence.

 "Grandpa," my grandson begins.

But I shush him.

"Let your soul drink it in." I say.

The boy follows my gaze

up to the evening sky,

all pierced with white dots,

while a round, Charlie Brown moon

touches the darkness

and shines its yellow beam

on the glasslike lake.

"God is here," I whisper.

 "Where?" he asks, frowning.

But then he sees my smile

and he understands

that we are in the Creator's workshop.

~ *four elements*

Earth, air, fire, and water—

the four elements of the universe.

All capable of energy

Earth—for gravity

Air—for flying

Fire—for heating

Water—for power

The power of water

is almost as ancient

as the earth itself.

Simple craft use oars

to ease boats forward

Grain mills use water

to drive the wheels

that crush granules

Electric plants use water

to turn the turbines

that give us energy

while the moon teases the sea

that gives poets

a way to describe the tide.

~ *thirst*

So runs the water

to quench our thirst.

Water once ran down the Jordan

to cleanse people from their sins.

It even cleansed One who knew no sin.

While a woman at Jacob's well drew water,

the Holy One offered her *living* water

so she would never thirst again.

~ *the dirt of memory*

So runs the water

from spigot onto hands

The coal miner,

The ditch-digger,

The homeless,

The forgotten.

All remove their dirt of memory.

Yet God's whisper

thunders in their ears,

reminding them that

the homeless,

the handicapped,

the heartsick,

are our brothers and sisters,

and He wants to welcome us home.

~ *leaves of grass*

So runs the water

over plots of thirsty leaves of grass.

Rather than leaves, however,

they are green, long, and

happy, praying hands,

shaved by mowers on mornings,

choked by weeds,

but otherwise ignored.

Nonetheless, these green hands

thank the clouds

for the rain,

for the soil,

and for the sun.

While grass dies

in the winter

it will rise again

in the spring

…like we all will

~ *sunlight*

Yes, we, like the sun will rise

even after a terrible night

Yes, we, like the Son, will rise

after our dreadful darkness.

*   *   *

The black evening churns into

light gray, then a happy yellow.

The risen sun spreads its warmth

across a cold seacoast in Maine

and directs a single golden ray

through a drab kitchen window,

where little Amelia weeps at the table.

Because Mommy went to heaven last night
Amelia's face is awash with tears.

The sun's light glistens her unkempt hair,
while the Son's light calms her despair.

~ *water lilies*

Floral bursts on water...

they so impressed Monet

he did 250 different paintings,

in a vain attempt to grasp their beauty.

Water lilies reflect

the sunset,

passing clouds,

pond stillness.

A floral dress covers her plain attire,

as if dressing her for the prom.

Maybe that is why

park-goers stare at them.

Maybe they expect

to have a conversation with water lilies.

And they do.

Sylvia Plath

wrote about water,

as did

Walt Whitman,

as did

many other poets who

found it mysterious, haunting.

Thus, so runs the water

as a babbling brook,

where poets reach into their bag of words

where artists reach for their paint pallet,

wishing to empty their souls.

Words hunger for the touch of a pen

held by drifting minds of poets.

They see a different vision,

not the vision of the material world.

With love, they caress the alphabet

and string its letters on a clothesline.

But discordant winds and a hot sun

torture springs into hopeful meanings,

straining to capture its substance

for more than the *science* of water.

They take up their pens again

to assemble yet more words.

Alas, they struggle

to massage their pen markings

into private thoughts

into a substance

only they can understand.

Some poets hope their readers

will not be distracted by

a sip of chardonnay,

a bit of goat cheese,

or the waiting lips of a lover--

while a poet's well-crafted words

begin to vanish like a mist.

~ my book of words

Water can be regulated,

channeled in its flow —

but not the words I seek.

53

They are like spoiled children,

running to and fro

in obvious disobedience.

Yet even my inspired words

garner public indifference.

Since you refuse to see my pain

I shall leave you, head bowed

so you may play your strident noise

while I open my book of words

to recount the sum of all my joys.

Words take wing like songbirds,

finding minds to touch and arouse,

where characters give love and reveal

imagined souls for me to browse.

Matters not if they be false or real.

   Pages press scenes within my heart

   and arrange my thoughts, part by part.

~a fountain of ideas

I am distracted for a moment,

observing how streams of water

soar like missiles toward the sky,

only to arch downward,

gravity dashing any hope for freedom.

Then I return to my writing class,

a collection of minds where we

focus on true or imagined

stories of love,

as we painfully sketch our

way to new insight,

and hang our varied thoughts

on a mere page!

I search for inspiration,

and through a window

I see that fountain, fountain,

Ah, *Fountainhead*,

and I am reminded of

Roark, Keating, and Tooney

in Ayn Rand's novel.

Her flashes of characters

sprinkled like the spatter

of bright colors on a large canvas...

emotions of despair, struggle,

and hints of tears and smiles.

But in my story, I realize

my characters have become

banal and boring,

like that fountain of water.

~ *history*

Water has a history,

going beyond the ancients.

So too, I hope the history

in all of us will ascend

into His giant Book of Life,

containing the secrets of our souls,

and the memories of our minds

Great writers mesh soul and heart

Word weavers open both

to get as close as they can

to undeniable truth.

~ *remembering*

Remember those days

when Google was not a verb,

when we could trust strangers,

when comedians avoided gutter jokes,

when gay people did not get married,

when we wrote letters instead of emails,

when we gave our children simpler gifts,

when the word "terror" was not used much,

when we'd go to a drive-in on Saturday nights,

when we believed that life began at conception,

when people shunned government handouts,

but most of all....

remember when we were in touch with God on

a daily basis?

Remember? I say, remember?

~ time curtain

Once I watched a surfer

conquer the Gulf of Mexico

by refusing to be upended.

I also refuse to be upended

by the present generation.

I want to think of Ahab calling Starbuck

not for a vanilla latte,

but to hasten the catch of the White Whale.

I want to think of Emily Dickinson talking

not on her smart phone,

but scratching her thoughts on paper.

I want to think of Nick Carraway

not tweeting Joe Gatsby

but using his own voice

to say he won't attend tonight.

My mind is tormented

by the internet,

where we can un-friend someone

with a finger click

or where we can reduce our thoughts

to a mere 140 characters.

I want to retreat to a faraway time

when Shakespeare was not

a fishing rod,

nor Dickens the name of a café,

nor Plato a soldering tip,

nor Amazon an online retailer

rather than a mighty river.

~ *time traveling*

So runs the water

boiling into steam

to run the Iron Horse

driving it far West.

So also runs the water

as a nineteenth century river

to guide a time traveler like me.

Yonder I see people pumping water

to quench livestock and themselves,

thanking God for colorless liquid gold.

~ memories as a youth

> So runs the water,
>
> and it carries memories for me,
>
> like the bathwater that ran
>
> while Mom checked its warmth
>
> before allowing me to step in,
>
> or like the rain that soaked
>
> me when I walked two miles
>
> from the library with no umbrella,
>
> or like Lake Michigan's waves
>
> wonderful to behold,
>
> but ever so cold in June.

~ pieces of past

> The old man reeled in his line.
>
> Maybe, he thought, he ought to try
>
> catching remnants of his past instead.
>
> So he drove a long ways
>
> and parked by an old cedar
>
> near a creek that used to be a river.

He took out his map of the area

and trudged a dusty road, searching.

A collie raced along, barking

while the man cursed it all—

the loud dog, useless map, and hot sun.

He could not find the barn with the

crushed roof nor the house with

sides mottled with paint flakes

nor the old cowshed

where he once spent the night

after Pa took a switch to him.

Gone too was the pond

where he would skinny dip on Saturdays,

and the dogwood bush he hid behind

when Becky showed up one day.

He had hoped to at least discover

his old schoolhouse farther up,

but a gas station now occupied

that plot, and pieces of his past

drifted before his eyes like leaves

falling across the lawns

of condominiums and a Shell station.

~ eternity

So runs the water,

waters of ancient Earth,

waters existing since Creation;

yet it seems like an eternity to me.

Time without end—I cannot fathom it.

Even so, I know I am deathless

and I will live on because my soul lives on,

and the living will search for answers,

while the dead will have already found them.

Nature gives me a clue to eternity.

The grass hides in the winter

but resurrects in the spring.

And those great souls who have lived,

Mozart, Plato, Tolstoy, and Rubens,

cannot just lie barren forever.

They have music to compose

and philosophy to study

and novels to write

and figures to paint.

~ *Nymphs*

Greek goddesses,

free and flowing,

dancing and singing,

to the rush and splash of water

from streams where they live,

unburdened by morals,

unburdened by mortals.

Coleman and Waterhouse

imagined them in water

unhampered by clothing,

personifying nature.

Others showed them

carefree and joyful.

But their joviality did not fool me

Their faces gave way to sadness,

awaiting,

hoping,

for the unattainable.

~ what if

What if Santiago

    never had his big catch?

What if Ahab

    never caught the white whale?

What if Caesar

    never crossed the Rubicon?

What if Bathsheba

    never showered outdoors?

What if Mitchell

    never got her novel published because

    she had placed her manuscript

    on a patio table facing Lake Seminole

    and a strong gust blew her pages away?

    Thus, if her book was gone with the wind

    would Scarlett still want Ashley?

    Would Melanie still cry?

    Would Rhett Butler still not

    give a damn?

~ laughing girl

The sea was made

for laugher and frivolity.

I see a little girl laughing in Oahu.

Laughing girl, laughing girl,

are you competing

with the sunshine?

or a happy swim in the sea?

or that sand castle you made?

Your neck is encircled with a lei

Thus you lead me to say

that I do find it odd

your bright beam of joy

reminds me of God.

~where is there?

Humpback whales swim to Hawaii

because warm climate is there.

Ships migrate toward a lighthouse

because the shore is there

There is something magical in "there".

Do you believe in Yahweh?

If you'll only open your eyes

you will see Him...There.

As sure as beauty or love exists,

He also exists...There.

Perhaps if He blew dandelion florets

into the autumn sky

you would know He is...There.

Or if He flew to the tallest chimney

and diverted away black smoke clouds,

you would know He is...There.

No Creator? Then how do you explain

the sweetness of newly-mown grass

or the sudden appearance of a newborn,

or the inspiring music of a composer—

like that of a Beethoven symphony?

His music can seep into the very endpoint

of our basic emotions, coexist

with the things we cherish the most,

and seduce us into a floating dream.

~ the killing fields

So runs the water

as rivers carrying the blood of martyrs.

Years ago a child named Amena loved dance.

A three-foot tall ballerina for her first lesson.

Click.

In teenage years she circled and hummed

and wore a white skirt for her first audition.

Click.

Now twenty, her feet swayed and she smiled.

A conservative black dress her first formal.

Click

Captured by ISIS, her feet kicked, she screamed

A wooden casket for her first eternity.

Click.

.

~ *fish*

Man was not made for the sea.

The sea was made for man.

If God gave us only minnows

we would be fed but bored.

Instead He gave us a variety

to wow us with His creativity.

The oceans, lakes, and rivers

abound with many species,

many colors,

many sizes,

many types.

Carp, haddock, bluefish,

swordfish, perch, and cod,

and thousands more He's made.

~ *gift-wrapped*

Caught my first trout

at a trout farm.

Now that I'm older

I buy it at the market.

Caught my first perch

at Lake Michigan

Now that I'm older

I buy it at the market.

Caught my first salmon

in the Pacific Ocean.

Now that I'm older

I don't buy it at the market.

I enjoy it with wine at Landry's.

But I wish that I had snorkeled

and seen varieties of fish close up.

Hmm... Actually, I *do* see them close up.

Yet I wonder what those fish think of me

when I ogle them—head, fins, and all,

through a protective glass window.

To a shark, I'm a big meal

To others, no big deal--

In fact, they ignore me

and swim away.

~ *until death do us part*

There is something admirable

about inseparability.

Like Ida and Isidore Strauss

standing near a lifeboat.

Others urged Ida to board it,

but she refused.

Turning to her husband Isidore

she said "Where you go, I go."

And the two of them sank

with the Titanic.

~ *breaking water*

A break from labor

A stress from work

A rest for water

A soothing fluid

Breaking water

Pain of labor

Must push harder

Cries from mother

Pain of labor

Cries from baby.

Pain's reward!

~ *relativity*

Everything is relative.

Cold water

as the only drink

offered to desert nomads

is praised.

Cold water

as the only drink

offered to rich diners

is cursed.

~*water's benefits*

A wonderful invention

by our intelligent Creator is

water.

It increases energy,

releases fatigue,

prevents cramps,

flushes out toxins,

boosts our immune system,

improves skin complexion,

maintains regularity,

hydrates our dehydration.

Water—our elixir of life.

~ *polluted waters*

So runs the water

once pure enough to drink

wholesome and chaste like a saint,

now, disappearing as our elixir of life.

No longer a healthy drink but a

yellow and rust-colored liquid in

the Sarno, Ganges, Citarum Rivers,

and many hundreds more.

Dead fish rotted long since,

poisoned by gluttonous factories

and used as public toilets.

Water, choked by chemicals,

strangled daily by filth.

Once a thing of beauty from God

now a cesspool for mankind.

~ *spiritual nourishment*

But I like to think of pure water

as I am lowered into its goodness

as a *spiritual* nourishment,

whence I am indeed born again

with the invocation of the Holy Spirit.

I like to think of heaven

with streams of *living* water,

flowing by the garden of my mansion

where I will be living in the Kingdom.

The Lord opened the waters

of the great Red Sea

At God's command Moses struck the rock

      at Meribah

to bring his doubters water.

Jesus changed water into wine

      at Cana

He offered living water to a Samaritan

at Jacob's well.

He commanded a blind man to wash

in the pool of Siloam

~ *souls run also*

So run human souls,

checking with self

to see if their actions

will feed their appetite

for kudos and reward.

Rare are those who

run the race blindly,

run each day for others

run like mighty rivers,

running because they want to,

dying because they have to.

More Water Reflections

Faith

    is like a mind set

    on still another sunrise

    over a mirrored lake

Hope

    is like a lifeguard

    who pulls you from the river

    so you can live tomorrow.

Love

    is like an awesome rainbow

    after your shipwreck

    from the anger of the sea.

Peace

    is like a walk to the pond

    after quarrels have abated

    and its stillness hugs you.

Under a Microscope

How does one study water?
In class we undressed the molecule
and peered at its nakedness
Two attractive hydrogen atoms
were caught kissing an oxygen atom.
With a sextillion of these marriages
we'd have a drop of water.

I did an electrolysis experiment
separating the two gases,
but then I marveled at how
fortunate we are that
two hydrogen atoms
did not kiss
two oxygen atoms
because hydrogen peroxide
would taste horrible.

A Baffling Situation

Academia worries about

the strangest things concerning water.

Like how fast do bubbles

of water rise to the surface?

Or, if you put baffles

in a heated tank of water

and run a propeller in it,

how does the number of baffles

affect the water's heat transfer?

Water plays a hide-and-seek game.

Oxygen and nitrogen atoms hide there,

and though you seek you cannot find them

unless you boil that water

and they bubble up,

revealing air's hiding place.

Tears

So runs a tear

down a quivering cheek

when he explodes

his wrath at her,

when a teenager

is enraged at her dad,

when a convict is told

he is not forgiven,

when a cheerless family

gathers at a gravesite.

It starts in the cerebrum

where sorrow is registered.

Yet tears are the manifestation

of the deepest grief of a soul.

We can buy tear drops

at a local pharmacy,

but we cannot buy real tears,

like those shed by Jesus

at the tomb of Lazarus.

Watering an Oak

A patch of summer
flashes on an ancient oak,
A dog appears, sniffing its bark
and peeing on its trunk
as if paying homage
and disrespect at the same time.
The tree does not mind
but months pass
and its leaves depart from its limbs,
as cruel winds undress it
for the coming winter,
when snow blankets its nudity.
But the oak is patient
and awaits the next spring
when a dog arrives to sniff its bark
and pee on its trunk
to pay homage and disrespect
once again.

Running Through

So runs the water

through hoses to douse a blaze,

and through cannons to douse rioters,

and through sprinklers to nourish grass,

and through straws to quell a thirst,

and through pipes to gives us showers.

So runs the water,

but it never tires of running.

The Ark

When the Lord saw evil abound,

He purged humankind with a flood,

save for Noah and his family.

It is thus wondrous to ponder

how the Ark of Noah

saved future generations,

how the Ark of Moses

contained the Law,

and how the Ark of Mary

carried the Word who saved us all.

The Influence of Water on History

Overcast skies, threat of rain,

saved Kukura from the Bomb,

while frost and snowstorms

saved Moscow from the Führer.

Hailstorms wiping out French crops

helped instigate the French revolution

 while the lack of severe weather

won D-Day for the world.

How interesting it is that

weather and *whether* sound the same

and in some historical settings

are close cousins.

The Sea in Classical Art

Leviathan

--a sea monster who battled Job

Whale

--the nemesis of Captain Ahab

Winslow Homer's "The Gulf Stream"

--Has the sailor drowned?

Edward Munch "The Scream"

--Has the body been found?

The Sea in Classical Music

"The Hebrides" by Mendelssohn

beauty of a water cave

"La Mer" by Debussy

misty, ghostlike seascape

"A Sea Symphony" by Williams

Walt Whitman set to music

"Une barque" by Ravel

sweeping melodies, peaceful ocean

Rivers

Each river has a story.

Each river has a history.

The Mississippi

a river painted in words,

in Mark Twain's stories.

The Klondike and Colorado

sites of the 1896 siege of gold.

The St. Lawrence

an Underground Railroad,

a haven for runaway slaves.

For me, it's the Kansas River,

quiet and unassuming.

But in an 1863 river town

it prevented Lawrence folks

from escaping Quantrill's fury.

Have a Glass of Ocean

Referring to the seas

At one time Coleridge was right:

"Water, water, everywhere

and not a drop to drink."

Maybe it's no longer true.

Our desalination projects

with reverse osmosis

may well reverse his thought.

Beach Memories

On Saturday mornings

our upstairs tenant

introduced me to Lake Michigan

by driving me there to fish.

Ten-year-old Tom, waiting on a pier

for sunrise and fish.

I, a young "old man of the sea",

waiting and waiting for the big one,

and it came—a two-pounder.

My parents, sister, and I went to the beach

on a streetcar I should have named *Desire.*

(I loved the clangs and screeching tracks.)

My parents never touched the water.

My sister ran her toes in it,

but I splashed about like a crazed dolphin,

then had to sit on a hot blanket

wondering why the sun

hated my skin.

Trees and Water

I never thought of a tree as a

hydraulic system or giant straw.

Yet because trees need water

they must somehow extract

water from the soil,

not only to the trunk

but up to the limbs,

and further up, way up

to the uppermost tree leaf.

It is the xylem vessels

which do all this work,

yet I am amazed at how tall redwoods

can nourish its leaves hundreds of feet up,

fighting gravity every inch of the way.

Well, I put my science book away

so I can admire the genius of our Creator.

The Sea Organist

There is something fascinating

yet annoying about those breakers.

As I lay on the beach

I hear a different pitch

with each crash of the sea.

It is as if each sweep of a wave

finds a different crevice to slam against.

The ocean is like an organist

stuck on somber music,

playing only low notes,

then booming into a crescendo,

as if showing off its power.

Yet, I want the sea organist

to cease trying to impress me

when I want to nap on the beach.

Mermaids

Shakespeare wrote about mermaids

As did Yeats, Eliot, and Wilde

While Greeks had their nymphs

the rest of the world

had their mermaids.

Half-woman, half-fish

They swam the waters

and lived in the sea.

I sometimes wonder

what I'd do if I caught one

while fishing at the pier.

 Maybe I'd keep her and

add her to my collection of

nymphs and unicorns

that I keep in my mind.

Thunder and Lightning

Lord, you woke me

at three in the morning,

flashing Your whiteness

and brightening my room.

Your banging on the sky

with explosive thunder

and streaking white lights

woke me at three in the morning.

You now have my attention.

What is it You want, Lord?

I don't believe for a second

that those pounding booms

 are mere sound waves

resulting from collapsing air

or that those flashes are just

clashing charges of static electricity

These are Your explosions,

designed to get my attention.

As I hear the rain ping my windows,

and more pounding, more flashing,

tell me what You want, Lord.

Snow

So runs the water

unless it runs no longer

because it is now frozen

and its crystals align

to make roads slippery

while forming icicles

hanging over roof ends,

or forming snowflakes,

so children can form angels,

or make snowmen,

or scan the white-dotted night,

searching for Santa on Christmas Eve.

Many Forms

So runs the water

unless it is boiled

so it becomes steam

and gives pleasure

to aches in steam rooms

and helps Mom

when she irons out

the wrinkles of our clothes,

but not the wrinkles of our memory.

Peculiar thing,

this substance called water.

It is more ancient

than we are.

We dive in it.

We float in it.

We sail over it.

We drink it.

Pilate washed in it

to remove his guilt,

The Baptist used it

to remove sin,

People bathe in it

to remove grime.

So runs the water

God's gift to us.

About the Poet

Tom Mach wrote three popular historical novels, *Sissy!* *All Parts Together*, and *Angels at Sunset*, all of which won awards. In addition, he wrote two children's books, *The Invisible Twins* and *The Adventures of Homer the Roamer*, both of which received 5-sar reviews and accolades from children. His poetry collection, *The Uni Verse*, won the 2008 Nelson Poetry Book Award. His poems were published in *Blue Island Review*, *Imagine* magazine, *Parnassus* magazine, the *International Library of Poetry*, *The Poet*, and other publications. His second poetry book, *The Museum Muse*, also received considerable praise from readers. In addition to winning poetry awards from the Kansas Authors Club, Tom was a finalist in a nationwide Writer's Digest Awards competition. His website is **www.Tom-Mach.com**